my first dog book

my first dog book

35 fun activities to do with your dog,
for children aged 7 years +

Dawn Bates

CICO kidz

For Zep and Poppy

Published in 2015 by CICO Books
An imprint of Ryland Peters & Small Ltd
20–21 Jockey's Fields, London WC1R 4BW
341 E 116th St, New York, NY 10029

www.rylandpeters.com

10 9 8 7 6 5 4 3 2

Text © Dawn Bates 2015
Design © CICO Books 2015
Photograph on page 18 by Mark Lohman © CICO Books 2015,
photograph on page 128 by Adrian Monagle © CICO Books
2015, all other photographs © Corbis Images 2015

A CIP catalog record for this book is available from the Library
of Congress and the British Library.

ISBN: 978 1 78249 197 2

Printed in China

Editor: Jane Birch
Series consultant: Susan Akass
Designer: Rosamund Saunders
Illustrator: Hannah George

In-house editor: Anna Galkina
In-house designer: Fahema Khanam
Art director: Sally Powell
Production controller: Sarah Kulasek-Boyd
Publishing manager: Penny Craig
Publisher: Cindy Richards

The author and the publishers cannot accept any legal
responsibility for any personal injury to dogs or children
arising from the advice and activities outlined in this book.
If your dog is unwell or has behavioral problems, always seek
the advice of a vet or other qualified dog expert.

Contents

Introduction

So you're getting your first dog? That's great news! Dogs make wonderful companions. They are by nature sociable, loving, and loyal creatures, and a great addition to any family. But they can only be all of these things if they have a good, responsible owner who meets their needs, both practical and emotional. This book helps you to maximize your dog's potential so that he can become the companion and friend you always imagined.

Your dog will become a great playmate but first you need to learn how to look after him. In Chapter 1, Caring For Your Dog, discover the essentials of dog care, from understanding his behavior and body language to exercising, house-training, and keeping him healthy.

No dog is perfect. Your dog will rely on you to teach him how to behave well. Chapter 2, Good Dog, covers all the basic training techniques, with easy step-by-step instructions, from sit, down, and fetch to walking to heel on the leash (lead). Discover how to solve problems such as play-biting and jumping up, and how to help your dog to behave well around people and other dogs.

Playtime will become much more fun with your new canine companion. In Chapter 3, Fun and Games, there are ideas for great activities to enjoy together such as Hidden treasures, Doggy soccer, and Tug-of-war. You can also learn how to make your own dog toys and set up an obstacle course.

It's great to show off your dog. In Chapter 4, Clever Dog, discover how to teach your pup some skilful tricks. Impress your friends by getting your dog to Roll over, Wave, or give a High-five with one simple command from you!

So get ready to enjoy this wonderful relationship. Your first dog will always hold a special place in your heart.

chapter 1
Caring for your dog

Preparing for your dog's arrival

When your family gets a dog you will be gaining a new playmate, companion, and friend but there will be some new responsibilities, too. Your dog will need to be walked daily, fed, groomed, and trained, —and don't forget, someone has to scoop up the poop! Start getting prepared before your dog arrives, and go shopping for all the things you will need.

A new member of the family

You and your family will need to work out how your dog will fit in with your daily and weekly routines. Sit down together and talk about her day-to-day care. Who will be responsible for walking her? How many times each day will she be fed and who will do this? Who will train her? If you're going to share the training, make sure you're all using the same techniques (see Chapter 2). It is worth drawing up a rota of jobs that can be ticked off once they've been completed.

Doggy shopping list

It's important that you have all the equipment you need by the time your dog arrives in her new home.

Collar and leash (lead): Most pet stores will be able to tell you whether to buy a small, medium, or large collar and leash, depending on the breed of dog you are getting. You can buy an ordinary leash or a retractable leash. Retractable leashes, which lengthen as your dog walks away from you, are not recommended for puppies and dogs that have not been trained to walk to heel (see page 66), so it is better to buy an ordinary one.

Many collars come with an identity tag that contains a piece of paper to fill in, or you can buy a tag to engrave and attach. In the UK, and in most states in the USA, it is the law that your dog must wear a dog identification tag on his collar. Write your name and address, including zip code (post code) on the paper, or get it engraved on a tag. Include your telephone number, as it makes it easier to contact you if your dog gets lost. Don't include the dog's name because, if someone tries to steal your dog, the thief may gain the dog's trust by calling him by name. It is also recommended that you have your dog microchipped (see page 14).

Food and drinking bowls: It is best to buy two of each. Choose a feeding bowl based on the breed of your dog and the amount she is likely to eat. You can buy special drinking bowls for breeds such as spaniels that have long ears. They are designed to keep their ears out of the water!

Dog food: There is a wide range of dog food available so find out what your dog needs, before she arrives, according to her age and breed. The more natural the food, the better, so avoid those that contain dyes and artificial preservatives. Look for food that provides a balanced and complete diet. Don't buy too much of one type of food to

Picking up poop

Picking up poop is something you will have to get used to when you get a dog. Here is how to do it:

When your dog poops, put one hand right inside a poop bag (see illustration, right).

Pick up the poop with the bag—make sure you pick up all of it.

Use your other hand to pull the bag inside out, making sure you don't touch the poop.

Tie the top of the bag in a knot and place it in a dog waste station (bin).

If you are out walking your dog, clean your hands thoroughly with an antibacterial handwipe or handwash straight after you have picked up the poop. If you are at home, wash your hands really well with warm water and antibacterial handwash or soap.

begin with, in case it doesn't suit your dog. Don't feed small bones, such as chicken bones, to your dog as these could splinter in her throat and might get stuck.

Training pads: These are absorbent pads you can buy from any pet store if your dog needs house-training (see page 30).

Poop bags: Buy plenty of poop bags and make sure you always take a few with you on walks. Be aware that the cheapest types are often the most flimsy—you get what you pay for.

Grooming supplies: When it comes to bathing and grooming your dog, you will need dog shampoo and a brush or comb The type you need to buy will depend on your dog's coat, so do some research beforehand. Buy your dog her own towel or set aside one or two old ones for her.

Using a crate

Dogs instinctively look for a den—a safe place to be—and this is what a crate provides. She should go in there to feel safe and comfortable so you should never use it as a way of punishing her. When you first get a crate, tempt her to go in there by using toys and treats. When she seems tired or when the house is very busy, encourage her to go into her crate because dogs, like humans, need down time.

Most dogs don't like to use their den as a toilet so a crate is also useful for house-training. A crate should be big enough for your dog to stand up in, turn around, and lie flat in, but not so big that she can use a part of it as a toilet. A dog can sleep in a crate at night but it is not right to leave your dog in a crate all day.

Bed (and a crate if you're planning to do crate-training; see the box, right): You want to ensure your dog is comfortable, but you don't have to buy an expensive bed. Remember, dogs originally lived in the wild and in many countries they still live outside! Also bear in mind that a puppy or a nervous, unsettled dog is likely to tear a new bed to pieces. If you don't want your dog to lie on the couch (allow it once and she'll do it all the time!), buy a bed or a blanket for the living room, too. Check the washing instructions on a dog bed before you buy it and buy one that is easy to wash.

Treats: Try to save treats for training (see Chapter 2) in the first few months. There are many packages of training treats on the market but you can also make your own by cutting up food such as cheese, cooked sausages, and cooked chicken into bite-sized treats. Make sure you don't give your dog too many treats as she may gain too much weight. If you have a puppy, add chew toys to your shopping list. Better she gnaws away at those than the furniture!

Toys: You don't need to buy toys for your dog but playing is a great way to bond with her and toys are also useful for training. Clear out your own toy box—there may be old soft toys or balls in there that you no longer play with, or why not get creative and make her some toys yourself (see page 82)?

! SAFETY FIRST

• Whether your new dog is a puppy or an older dog, she should be booked in for a health check with a vet the week she arrives. When you get a new dog, you should be given her medical history, such as whether her vaccinations are up to date. If for any reason you don't know this, get advice from your vet.

• The vet will also be able to microchip your dog. This quick and simple process involves implanting a microchip under your dog's skin so that she can be identified and returned home if she becomes lost. It is worth doing this even though she already wears an identity tag.

• If your dog pulls when being walked, consider buying a harness. You attach the leash to the harness instead of to a collar. This may give you more control and will take the strain off your dog's neck when she pulls.

Dogs in cars

As part of your family, your dog will need to travel, but there are some important tips to remember before you take her in your car.

Just as you have a car seat and wear a seat belt in a car, so your dog should be restrained when traveling in a car. This will stop her jumping around and distracting the driver, but will also help prevent injuries to your family and the dog in an accident. To restrain a dog you could use a dog harness attached to a seat belt, a dog crate—you can use her normal crate or buy a special travel one—or, in a station wagon (estate car), a partition between the load area and back seat.

● Dogs should always travel in the back seat because it is less distracting for the driver and because, if an airbag goes off in an accident, this could badly injure your dog.

● Make regular stops on long journeys at safe places, away from traffic, to let your dog out and offer her a drink of water.

● Never let your dog stick her head out of the car window—it is dangerous.

● It is dangerous to leave a dog alone in a stationary car, even for a few minutes. A car left in the sun heats up like an oven and panting will not cool a dog down enough.

● Be careful when letting your dog out of the car near traffic. Hold onto her collar or leash to stop her running into the road.

● Always remember to carry water and a drinking bowl for your dog in the car

Getting to know your dog

The more you get to know your dog, the better the care you can provide. You'll soon get to know your dog's character—both the good sides and the bad—and you will be able to predict how she will behave in different situations. It can help if, from the very beginning of your relationship, you try to see things from a dog's point of view.

1 She's not a human

Although dogs love humans and your dog will soon become part of your family, it is important to remember that she isn't human. She isn't as clever as you and doesn't think in the same way and, although you can develop a way to communicate with your dog, she doesn't speak your language. So bear all this in mind and don't expect too much too soon. Learn her doggy body language and try to understand her moods. (see page 20).

2 She's not a toy or an accessory

Let's face it, most dogs are adorable. Puppies, especially, are like real-life cuddly toys. Who wouldn't want to pick them up and cuddle them? Although your dog will enjoy some cuddles, don't try to hold her all the time. Dogs are meant to spend most of their time on all fours, not in your arms or, even worse, in a purse (handbag)! Better to sit next to your dog and stroke her or allow her to sit or lie next to you, as she would if she was in a pack of dogs, than to carry her around.

3 Her senses are very different

Smell: Your dog is led by her nose. While you might check out your surroundings by looking at everything, your dog will do the same by sniffing. Be aware of this and allow your dog to investigate with her nose, especially when she first arrives in her new home. She'll soon sniff out food if you leave it lying around the house, so don't tempt her into stealing by doing this. She'll also depend on scent to investigate new people and dogs (especially their bottoms). You mustn't get cross with her for following her instincts!

Hearing: You might sometimes see your dog jump up, prick up her ears, and bark. She's probably heard something that you haven't because she has much better hearing than you and can hear high-frequency sounds that you aren't able to detect. Having said that, good hearing doesn't mean she will listen to you. She's more likely to watch your hand signals than hear your words, so bear this in mind when you begin training (see Chapter 2).

Sight: Overall your dog's sight isn't as good as your own, but she can see better at night. She can't see detail or color in the same way as you. She can only see blues and yellows, not reds and greens. So if you throw a tennis ball onto the grass, she'll track it down with her nose rather than with her eyes.

She's a pack animal

Dogs naturally live in packs and this affects their behavior. First, it means your dog won't like to be alone for long periods or, possibly, not at all. Think about her day-to-day routine and try to ensure she isn't by herself for long stretches of time. Let her make friends with other dogs and people (see page 76) as much as possible and allow her to spend as much time with you as she can.

Second, the pack instinct means your dog will look for a leader. She will expect that person to give her some sort of routine and rules to guide her behavior. You need to be that person and to set the rules. If you don't, she may become worried and fearful or, worst of all, try to be the leader herself, which means she will become a badly behaved dog that controls your household.

5

She needs you

The relationship you have with your dog is essential to her development. Like any relationship, it won't always be perfect, but you must always try to be positive, patient, and kind to your dog. Once you have gained her trust and respect, she'll want to please you and you can look forward to many, many happy days together.

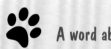 ### A word about friends

If you have a puppy, all your friends will want to meet her, but make sure you manage play dates carefully. Only invite one or two friends at a time. Allow them each to hold your puppy for a few minutes and to give her some treats. Make sure they handle her carefully and put her down on the ground gently, rather than dropping her from a height. If your puppy seems overwhelmed or frightened, cut the play date short. Warn them that your puppy will play-bite and explain what they should do (see page 74).

If your new dog is an older dog, always ask an adult to be there when your friends visit, as her behavior may be more unpredictable than that of a puppy, especially if you don't know her full history. Again, only invite one or two friends over at a time and don't overwhelm your dog.

Did you know?

A dog has 200 million cells in her nose to detect scent, compared to the 5 million you have!

Your dog's body language

Dogs communicate with each other by using body language and your dog will try to use this very same language to communicate with you. She can't tell you what she wants, or how she's feeling in words, so help her out by learning to read the signals.

Signs of stress

Your dog may do one or all of the following if she is anxious:

- Lick her lips continuously
- Yawn
- Turn away
- Tuck her tail between her legs

What to do: If you notice any of these signs, give your dog plenty of space. If necessary, gently guide her out of the stressful situation she is in.

Licking lips

Yawning

Turning away

Signs of unhappiness and intolerance

If your dog feels threatened or very uncomfortable, she will signal this. Growling and baring teeth are usually warning signs but do not necessarily mean she will bite. If the hairs on her backbone from her neck to her tail stand on end this is called raised hackles and is a sign she is on high alert. Look out for:

- Crouching
- Baring her teeth
- Ears back against her head
- Raised hackles
- Staring or narrowed eyes

What to do: Stay away from your dog and seek adult help. Make sure you back away slowly, and that you don't run.

Baring teeth

Ears back

Narrowing eyes

Raising hackles

Crouching

Signs of happiness and contentment

If all your dog's needs are met and she feels comfortable and content, you should mainly see the following body language:

- A relaxed posture
- A waggy tail (see the box opposite)
- Relaxed ears
- Lying on her back

What to do: Keep doing more of the same!

Lying on back

Did you know?

If your dog looks away when you stare at her, it's because she's trying to avoid confrontation, so don't get cross with her for being rude!

Relaxed posture

Upright tail

Tell-tale tail

Always judge your dog by her overall body language, rather than just a waggy tail. A stiff, upright tail that is moving from side to side, but not very wide, may signal that your dog is on high alert and not quite in a friendly zone. Very fast, frantic wagging may signal distress rather than contentment. If your dog is relaxed, her tail will be positioned level with her body, or slightly lower.

Exercising your dog

Walkies! Hearing this word is likely to make your dog very excited. Dogs need to be active. A dog that is exercised regularly will be happy, healthy, and well behaved.

Dogs are meant to walk, run, and explore in open spaces. In the past, dogs weren't bred to be house pets and sleep most of the day. They had physical jobs such as hunting or rounding up farm animals. Dogs naturally have a lot of energy and they need an outlet for it. An inactive dog that is shut up in a house will be bored, gain weight, and misbehave. Letting a dog out into the yard (garden) to run around doesn't count as exercise either. She needs a playmate—someone to encourage her to run and play. Who better to do that than you!

Make exercising your dog part of your daily routine. Walking and enjoying physical play together is a great way to bond and it will keep you fit and healthy, too.

SAFETY FIRST

When walking your dog you must think about your own and your dog's safety. Here is a list of tips to follow:

• An adult should always go with you when you are taking your dog for a walk. When you are older, if you are allowed to walk your dog on your own, always ask an adult first and tell them where you are going.
• If you cannot control your dog because she is too strong for you, or will not obey your commands, make sure that an adult holds the leash.
• Do not let your dog off the leash unless you are certain she will come back when you call.
• Try to find places that are away from traffic to exercise your dog.
• If you are walking your dog on dark mornings or evenings, wear some reflective clothing so that drivers can see you.
• If you are walking your dog in the countryside, remember to close gates and keep your dog away from farm animals. If you have to walk through a field of farm animals, always keep your dog on the leash.
• Always remember to take several poop bags with you.
• On long walks, make sure your dog has somewhere she can drink or take some water and a bowl with you. You can buy portable bowls that aren't too big or heavy to carry.
• On hot days, try walking your dog in the morning before the weather becomes too hot or in the late afternoon once it has cooled down a little.
• If you know your dog likes to swim, be careful when walking her near water. Never enter the water to help a dog.

1 Taking your dog for a walk

Try to walk your dog at least once a day, though puppies shouldn't be taken on long walks (see the box, right).

 **Puppy play**

Even you might find it hard to keep up with a puppy's boundless energy and demands for yet more fun and games. Most puppies need three 20-minute sessions of very active play per day. They shouldn't be walked for long periods of time because it may damage their soft joints and bones. If you know someone else with a puppy, arrange a play date. The two pups will chase each other, play fight, and roll around—and soon be fast asleep.

2 Playing fetch

Teach your dog to fetch (see page 60) a ball or her favorite toy. Fetching the toy and bringing it back to you will keep her fit and help her learn to obey orders. If it's raining or snowing or you don't have much outdoor space, throw a toy up and down the stairs. This will be a fantastic workout for your dog.

SAFETY FIRST

• Never throw sticks for your dog and don't let her play with sticks as they could splinter and get stuck in her throat, causing serious injury.

3 Chasing

Tie a piece of string to one of your dog's toys. Pull the toy along the ground, encouraging your dog to chase after it. After a few minutes, let her catch the toy but then teach her to drop it (see page 64). Some dogs enjoy a similar chase game using their leash.

4 Obstacle course

See page 88 to find out how to make an obstacle course for your dog, with tunnels and jumps. Setting this challenge is a great way to exercise her physically and mentally. Time how long it takes her to do one circuit and encourage her to go faster each time.

Did you know?

Dogs pant when they are excited but the more usual reason for panting is to cool down. Dogs are not able to sweat as well as humans, so when they are hot they pant—this lets out some body heat and lets in some cool air. If your dog is panting during exercise, stop the activity, move her to a cool place, and give her water to drink.

House-training

If you have a puppy, one of your main jobs in the early days and weeks will be teaching her where to pee and poop. She will need to go to the toilet often and must be trained to go outside. This job requires patience and kindness; remember that there are bound to be a few accidents.

1 **Take her outside regularly:** Until you recognize the signs that your puppy needs to go to the toilet (see Reading her body language, opposite), it's safest to take her outside as often as possible. Always go outside with her first thing in the morning and get an adult to take her outside last thing at night. Aside from this, take her outside when she wakes up after a sleep and after she eats. You are aiming for every hour or two during the day so the whole family will need to help with this job.

At night time, using a crate (see page 13) will reduce the chances of your puppy going to the toilet because she won't want to do this in the area in which she eats and sleeps. You may want to put down toilet-training pads but don't use these for too long because your puppy will assume this is where you want her to go and won't learn to go outside.

 2 **Find a toilet spot:** Encourage your puppy to pee and poop in the same spot outside, each time. Gradually, she will follow the scent and know that this is her toilet.

! **SAFETY FIRST**

• Keep plenty of poop bags to hand and always thoroughly wash your hands with an antibacterial handwash or soap after cleaning up after your dog (see page 12).

3 **Patience and rewards:** Once you're at the toilet spot, allow your dog to sniff around for a few minutes. Stay with her as, the more relaxed she is, the more likely she is to toilet. If you go back indoors, she is likely to follow you and not go to the toilet. Reward her with a treat when she pees or poops outside, then enjoy some playtime with her. She will associate going to the toilet outside as a very positive experience and know she has pleased you. If she does have accidents in the house, don't punish her. Remember, she's only young and is still learning.

Reading her body language

Look for the following signs that your puppy wants to go to the toilet. (She will have very little control of her bladder and bowel so you'll need to keep checking on her and then act fast!)

- Sniffing the ground
- Circling
- Crouching
- Pacing around the door to get outside

Older dogs

If you have an older dog who is not house-trained, try the puppy technique outlined here. If this doesn't work, you will need advice from a dog trainer or vet.

Did you know?

Dogs are instinctively clean animals and unlikely to want to toilet in a clean living area. If your dog has a toileting accident indoors, the area needs to be thoroughly cleaned for hygiene reasons and so that the scent has gone. If your dog smells the scent, she may think that this is her toileting area.

Bathing and grooming

It's bathtime! Your dog's bathing and grooming sessions should be an enjoyable experience for both of you. They are times for you to be physically close and bond, as well as an opportunity for you to keep your dog's coat in good condition.

A helping hand

It's probably going to be easier to bathe and groom a King Charles Spaniel than a Great Dane, so the amount of help you need may depend on the breed of dog you have, her size especially. It may also depend on her behavior and her tolerance levels.

If your dog is a puppy, get her used to being groomed and bathed from an early age. Ask an adult to help you for the first few times you bathe her and then you may be able to do this on your own. However, as she grows you may find you need help again.

If your new dog is fully grown, she may not like the process of being bathed and groomed because of a bad experience in the past. Always groom her with an adult present at first and be patient. Hopefully, in time, she will learn to enjoy it. If she doesn't, there are many professional groomers who are experienced in handling reluctant dogs.

You will need:

- Dog shampoo
- Your dog's towel
- Treats
- Dog brush or comb

Tips

- Put a rubber mat in the bathtub to stop your dog from slipping. This will make her feel more secure.

- Dress in old clothes. You are going to get wet and covered in dog hair!

- You may need to choose a shampoo that is particularly suited to your dog's coat.

- Have everything you need to hand before you begin.

- Keep bathtime short and fun for your dog. It should always be a positive experience.

- Bathe and groom your dog once she has been exercised. A tired dog will be much easier to handle.

- If your dog doesn't like having water on her face, use a washcloth to clean this area instead.

- When you take your dog out of the bathtub, she is likely to want to shake off the water. Allow her to do this and be prepared for a soaking! Even after being dried, she is likely to roll around to get dry. Make sure that she does this inside and not outside, otherwise it will be bathtime all over again!

- Shut the bathroom door before you start!

Bathing your dog

1 Brush your dog. If she is long-haired and her fur is easily matted, it is best to get any knots out before you bathe her.

2 Fill a bathtub with lukewarm water up to the level of your dog's elbows.

3 Place your dog in the bathtub. Get an adult to help if you can't lift her alone.

4 Thoroughly wet your dog's fur with lukewarm water. Either use a shower attachment, if there is one on the bath, or use a large plastic bowl to pour water over her. Be particularly careful when wetting your dog's face. Just like you, she is unlikely to enjoy having water poured or sprayed over her head! Give her a treat and praise her once you've completed this step.

5 Massage shampoo into her body using small circular movements and paying particular attention to any dirty areas. Give her a treat for good behavior.

6 Rinse off the shampoo, again taking great care around her face. Make sure all the shampoo has been thoroughly rinsed off. If it hasn't, your dog's skin is likely to become very itchy. Give her another treat after rinsing.

7 Lift your dog out of the bathtub, again asking for help if necessary. Thoroughly towel-dry your dog. You can also blow-dry her using a cool setting on the hairdryer. Once she's all dry, give her a treat.

Did you know?

When a dog shakes to get dry, it is an instinctive survival technique. Being wet makes a dog heavier, which makes it more difficult for her to run and escape danger.

Grooming

Brushing your dog's fur doesn't have to be a big event. It's something you can do while she's lying or sitting next to you. The more relaxed an experience it is, the more she is likely to enjoy it. Keep treats to hand and reward her during and after grooming. Try to make time to groom your dog regularly—at least once a week or more, depending on her type of coat.

1 Make sure you have brushes and combs that are suited to your dog's fur.

2 Be gentle, so that she feels as if she is being stroked with the brush or comb. Always brush from the roots to the tips, following the direction of the fur.

3 Gently unknot any tangles in your dog's fur.

4 Now enjoy some cuddle time with your newly pampered pooch.

10 ways to keep your dog healthy

Use this checklist to ensure your dog stays healthy and happy.

1 Choose the right food: Your dog needs a well-balanced, nutritious dog food that is free of dyes and artificial preservatives. Check the ingredients to ensure the food has a high meat and vegetable content and isn't just full of fillers such as corn and other grains. Good foods will be more expensive but are much healthier for your dog. Also, remember to buy a food that is just right for your dog's age because a young energetic dog will require different food to an older, less active dog.

2 Keep her hydrated: Your dog should be able to drink any time she wants to. Check and refresh her water bowl regularly and make sure it is clean. Take water and a bowl with you when you're out in hot weather or if you're going on a particularly long walk. Always take water for your dog on car journeys.

3 **Keep a check on her weight:** Dogs are greedy! Your dog may eat as much food as you are willing to give her. While feeding her might win her affection, overfeeding will only make her gain too much weight, and lead to her becoming less energetic and unhealthy. Measure her portions of food according to the package guidelines and keep treats to a minimum. They should only really be used for training purposes or very rarely as a reward. Do not feed your dog from the dinner table as this will encourage her to beg for food. If you do give your dog any left-over table scraps, be aware of the foods that can harm her (see the box on page 40). Be aware of the correct weight for your dog's size and age and ask your vet if you have any concerns about her weight.

SAFETY FIRST

• Always let your dog eat in peace and don't approach her or try to take her food bowl away while she is still eating. Dogs can try to protect their food and she might bite you if she thinks you are trying to steal it.

4

Get her immunized: Just like you, your dog should be immunized (given shots/injections/ vaccinations) to stop her getting certain illnesses which could be fatal. A puppy should be taken to the vet to be immunized twice, usually at around 6—8 weeks and then at 10—12 weeks. A puppy shouldn't mix with unvaccinated dogs until she has had all her immunizations, but it is important that she learns to socialize with other healthy, vaccinated dogs and with people before 12 weeks of age. Ask your vet for advice as to when it is safe for your puppy to start mixing with other dogs. Following their puppy vaccinations, dogs require a yearly booster shot to keep their immunizations up to date. This appointment is also a good opportunity for the vet to carry out a general health check.

5

Spot the signs of illness: A change in your dog's behavior and eating habits may mean she is ill. Always ask a vet if you think your dog is unwell. She may:
- Be off her food or drinking more or less water than usual
- Be less alert and playful
- Cry when you stroke her or try to pick her up
- Have sickness and/or diarrhea or be in discomfort when toileting
- Have lumps, swelling, or bleeding
- Be constantly coughing or sneezing
- Be unable to walk normally because of dizziness or a leg injury

6

Prevent fleas: It's easy to prevent your dog from getting fleas by applying a treatment to the back of her neck. Follow the instructions on the package for how often to do this and ask an adult to help when applying the treatment. You will be able to buy a better treatment from a vet than from a pet store. If your dog already has fleas, you may notice her scratching, chewing, and licking her skin all the time. You might see dark flecks on your dog's skin. If you suspect fleas, take your dog to the vet.

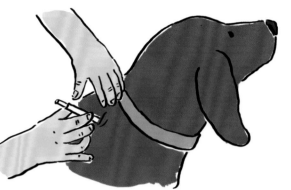

7

Prevent worms: Worms, which live inside dogs, can cause them to become ill, so you need to give your dog worming medication to get rid of them. Worms can come out of your dog in her poop and cause serious disease in people, so you should never touch any dog poop with your bare hands. If you do touch any poop accidentally, always make sure you wash your hands thoroughly as soon as possible. The amount of worming medication your dog should be given depends on her weight, so always get her weighed and then follow the guidance on the packaging. It is better to purchase a worming treatment from a vet rather than a pet supply store.

! SAFETY FIRST

• Always take an adult with you when you are purchasing flea and worming medication for your dog. An adult should also supervise you applying and using these treatments on your dog.
• An adult should always accompany you to veterinary appointments.

8

Look after her teeth: Just like your own teeth, your dog's teeth need regularly cleaning. They get a build-up of tartar that can cause gum disease and other problems. You can buy special dog toothpastes and toothbrushes to clean your dog's teeth. Regular chomping on rubber toys and chews made of rawhide will also help keep her teeth clean or you can buy her specially designed dental chews. Allow an adult to clean your dog's teeth and ears first. Once you're both confident she is happy with the processes, you can take over, but with an adult watching to begin with.

A deadly diet

The following are all harmful to a dog:

- Alcohol
- Avocado
- Bones, especially chicken bones
- Chocolate
- Garlic
- Grapes
- Medication designed for humans
- Macadamia nuts
- Onions
- Potatoes
- Raisins
- Raw eggs, meat, and fish
- Salty food
- Sugary food and drinks

9   **Look after her ears:** Your dog's ears will need to be cleaned regularly. Purchase a cleaning solution from your vet and follow the instructions that come with the product.

10   **Exercise her:** Daily exercise is essential to your dog's wellbeing (see page 26). Make taking her for a walk a priority and enjoy lots of physical play sessions together.

chapter 2

Good dog

Training your dog

A well-trained dog is quite simply a better companion and easier and safer to take out, so it's worth you and your family doing some basic training. If your dog understands what's expected of him and knows that you're in charge, he will be more contented and well behaved. Training sessions are a great way to stimulate your dog and, as they usually involve treats, praise, and your full attention, should be an enjoyable activity for your pooch. As you see your dog's behavior improve, it will become rewarding for you, too, but it will be hard work and you mustn't expect results too quickly.

Here are seven steps to successful training:

1

Keep sessions short: Make training sessions no longer than five minutes. Concentrate on one technique at a time. As your dog begins to learn and becomes responsive, you can make sessions slightly longer but always end them if your dog seems bored or tired. Follow training with some playful fun, if your dog isn't too tired, and lots of praise. Even if your dog has failed, praise him for trying his best.

2

Stock up on treats: The best way to train a dog is to reward him with treats. A treat doesn't need to be large—a thumbnail-size piece will do. The more "high value" (your dog will always enjoy a meaty treat more) and tasty the treat, the more likely your dog is to obey your commands—try cheese, cooked sausages, or ready-made packages of dog treats. Once fully trained, your dog will just do as you ask and won't look for a treat as a reward.

3 Choose the right time: A very energetic dog will be difficult to train. Take your dog for a walk or play in the yard (garden) with him before you start a training session. And, if you are too tired or just aren't in the mood for training your dog, find another time.

4 Choose different places: To begin with train your dog in a room where you are unlikely to be disturbed so that you can both concentrate. However, as your dog begins to learn, it's important to practice the same technique in different places. For example, if you only teach him to Sit beside his feeding bowl when he is waiting to be fed, he may not understand the same command beside the front door. Also, begin to practice the techniques with other people in the room or when you are out walking your dog.

5 **Be consistent:** There are different ways of teaching your dog the same thing. Choose one technique and make sure your whole family sticks to it, otherwise your dog may become confused about what's expected of him. Always use the hand signals as well as one clear word or short phrase. Your dog will learn more from what he sees than what he hears and he won't understand long sentences!

6 **Be positive:** Your dog won't always get it right but don't get angry with him when he fails. Look for the positives and praise him for what he has achieved rather than getting cross with him for what he hasn't understood. Your dog will value your attention and approval as much as he values the treats.

Using a clicker

A clicker is a small hand-held device used for dog training. Each time your dog does what you've asked, you "click," then give a treat. The dog soon learns that the sound of the click means you like what he's doing. The advantage of a clicker is that you can respond immediately to good behavior, but the disadvantage is that you may not always have it to hand. The training sessions in this book don't include the use of a clicker, but, if you want to, you can easily use one with the techniques given.

7

Be patient, persevere, and practice:
Not even professionals can train a dog overnight. It will take your dog time to learn the techniques that bring him rewards, so don't expect too much too soon.

Did you know?

In the wild, dogs travel in packs and there is always a leader. If you don't make yourself head of the pack, your dog will become the pack leader and try to rule you and your family!

Tips

• Look for a dog-training class in your neighborhood. This is a good way to learn directly from a professional and get advice if you are struggling with any part of training or behavior. There's the bonus that your dog will get to socialize with other dogs, too (see page 76).

• Work with the rest of your family so that you are all using the same techniques and commands to train your dog. It's an important part of the learning process for him to receive the same messages from everyone he lives with.

• Once your dog is trained in the basics, you can start adding in some impressive tricks (see Chapter 4), but in the early days don't show off your training techniques in front of other people. Your dog is likely to be confused if you expect him to "perform."

Getting your dog's attention

Your dog will only learn if he watches and listens to you. So the first step of training is getting him to pay attention. Don't worry, though, once you have a treat in your hand he'll learn this pretty quickly!

1 With your dog standing or sitting in front of you, say his name and "Look" (you may have to say it several times). Once he makes eye contact with you, say "Good boy" and give him a treat immediately.

2 Now repeat step 1, but once your dog makes eye contact, keep looking him in the eye and count to five before giving the treat.

3

This time, count to ten and then give the treat. It will take time to build up to longer periods of eye contact but eventually you will be able to get your dog's attention and eye contact without using treats.

Tips

• If your dog isn't being attentive, try using a higher-value, more meaty treat, so instead of a dog biscuit, give a piece of chicken or sausage.

• Try practicing getting your dog's attention when you're walking him. As you're strolling along, say, "Look at me." When he looks up, give him a treat. This is especially useful if your dog tends to get easily distracted on walks.

Teaching your dog to sit

Start training your dog by teaching him to sit. In a sitting position, you will have more control over him and he will be more likely to listen to your commands. Using the command "Sit" can be a useful way to calm down an excitable dog and stop him jumping up.

1 Get your dog's attention with a treat. Once he is standing in front of you, hold the treat near to his nose so that he can smell it.

2 Slowly move the treat toward the top of his head. As he follows the scent with his nose and raises his head up, his back legs will naturally move into a sitting position.

3 Once he is sitting, praise him by saying "Good boy" and give him the treat as a reward.

Tips

• Don't hold the treat too high. Your dog is likely to jump up to get it.

• Begin teaching this simple command in a quiet place, such as at home. Once your dog has mastered it, try instructing him to "Sit" when there are distractions, such as when you are walking him or at someone else's house.

4 Once he has learned to sit, start giving the voice command "Sit" before you begin steps 1—3. Also use a simple hand signal, such as the one shown here. With your palm facing upward, move your hand up toward your shoulder in one swift movement. Eventually your dog will respond to just the voice command or the hand signal, without the need for a treat, and sit in an instant.

! SAFETY FIRST

• Teach your dog to sit while you are waiting to cross the road. If he is sitting, you will have more control over him and he is less likely to step into the road ahead of you.

• Don't push on a dog's lower back, or pull a leash upward, to make him sit. Pushing may harm the dog, especially if he is a puppy.

Teaching your dog to lie down

As with Sit, being able to command your dog to lie down is a good way to control him, and it will calm him down if he's excitable. Make sure you have mastered the Sit command before you move on to Down.

Choose a quiet place to teach your dog to lie down. Remember that he may feel unsafe in a lying-down position, so give him lots of praise, affection, and reassurance.

1 First command your dog to sit, using the technique on pages 50—51.

2 Once he is sitting, hold a treat under his nose but don't give it to him yet.

3 Gradually lower your hand toward the ground and say "Down." Your dog's nose should follow the treat. You may have to move the treat along the floor away from your dog to get him to lie down properly.

4 Once he is lying down, feed him the treat, and praise him. If he stays lying down, give him another treat.

5 Eventually, pointing to the floor using a hand signal, such as the one shown here, should be enough to make your dog lie down.

Tips

• A dog feels that he is in a weak position when lying down. Don't attempt to make your dog lie down in a place where he may feel threatened, such as where there are other dogs, or people he doesn't know.

• Make it comfortable. Practice the Down technique on your dog's soft bed so that he gets comfort as well as treats!

• If your dog won't lie down, try sitting on the floor with your knees up and tempting him under your knees, so that he has to lie down to get the treat.

• Don't confuse your dog by saying "Down" when, for example, you want him to get off a piece of furniture. Choose the word "Off" instead.

Teaching your dog to wait

An obedient dog will wait when told to. This can be useful in lots of different situations, such as when you are preparing his food, if you don't want him to follow you from room to room, and when you need to control him off the leash.

Your dog can be taught to wait in a Sit or Down position. It is difficult to teach an excitable and energetic dog to wait, so practice this training technique once you have exercised him. Choose a quiet spot where he's unlikely to get distracted and fail!

1 Tell your dog to "sit". Stand directly in front of him, give the hand signal, as shown here, and say "Wait."

2 Count five seconds and, if your dog has remained still, give him a treat. If he has moved, try step 1 again.

! **SAFETY FIRST**
• Don't instruct your dog to wait in dangerous places, such as near a busy road.
• If your dog travels in a car, always teach him to wait when the car door is opened.

3 With your dog still sitting, slowly take a step back from him. From your new position, give the hand signal again and say "Wait." Count five seconds. Step forward and give him the treat.

Tips

• Gradually increase the time your dog has to wait and the distance from which you instruct him.

• Keep your hand signals slow, as a fast movement might excite him and cause him to move.

• Keep Wait training sessions short as they aren't that much fun for your dog!

• Always take the treat to your dog rather than calling him to you. He has to learn that by waiting he gets a reward.

Come when called

Once you and your family are confident your dog will come back when called, he can be allowed more freedom off the leash. This will mean more exercise for him and more enjoyable walks for you.

As with most aspects of training, having a tasty treat for your dog is the key to getting him to come to you. Eventually, he will come whether or not there is a reward on offer. Two of you will need to work together for this training technique.

1 One of you will need to gently hold your dog by the collar. Show your dog a tasty treat. Let him sniff it.

2 Take a few steps back from your dog, crouch down, and hold your arms wide open. Your body language should be open and inviting—your dog will follow your movements as well as your words.

3 Call your dog's name. This is a signal for your helper to let go of him.

4 When your dog approaches you, hold out the treat. If he doesn't come right up to you, gently guide him to you by holding his collar.

5 Give him the treat and lots of praise.

SAFETY FIRST

• Always teach your dog this training technique in your house or in an enclosed outdoor space, such as your yard (garden). Don't try it on walks until you are sure he will come to you.
• The first few times you let your dog off the leash outside the home, make sure that it is in a safe outdoor space away from roads, rivers, and other dogs.

Tips

- Make your call firm but enthusiastic.
- If your dog seems reluctant to come, try changing the treat you are offering to something more tempting.
- Gradually move farther away from your dog each time.
- If your dog is sniffing something or is playing with another dog, he may not always come immediately. Try to stay calm and patient, rather than running over to your dog and pulling him away. With the right treats on offer, he should come to you eventually.
- Coming to you should always be a positive experience so always praise your dog and give him a treat when he comes to you. Never tell him off or withhold a treat even if he has been slow to come.

Teaching your dog to fetch

As well as being a useful training technique, fetch (or "retrieve") is also a fun game for both of you. Until your dog learns to bring the toy back, expect to have to do a fair amount of running around yourself!

For your game of Fetch (or Retrieve), choose your dog's favorite toy or ball. Get him very excited about it. Make sure he really wants it! Eventually, he will jump around and bark in anticipation as soon as you pick it up. It can help to hide the toy for a while before playing Fetch to make your dog want the toy even more.

Running after the toy

1 Start by showing your dog the toy. Wave it around in front of him until you are sure he is keen to hold it.

2 Once his full attention is on the toy, throw it and tell him to "Fetch."

SAFETY FIRST

• Some dogs are very possessive about their toys. Never try to grab the toy from your dog's mouth. Your dog has to be willing to let go.

3 When he has picked up the toy, walk over to him, praise him, and stroke him. If he drops the toy, encourage him to hold it again.

Don't expect your dog to bring the toy back right away. Spend several sessions getting him to run after the toy before you start teaching him to bring it back to you.

Bringing the toy back

1 Follow steps 1—3 on the opposite page. Once your dog has picked up the toy, walk backward away from him, encouraging him to walk toward you with the toy.

2 Stop after a few steps. When your dog reaches you, encourage him to drop the toy in exchange for a treat. Say "Drop it" (see pages 64—65). As soon as he releases the toy, give him the treat and plenty of praise.

Move farther away from your dog each time you try this. After a while, you won't have to move from the spot where you threw the toy. Your dog will fetch the toy and bring it straight back to you.

Tips

• If you are using a ball to play Fetch but can't throw very far, use a ball launcher. This makes it easy to throw a ball a long distance with a simple flick of the wrist. Another way is to hit the ball using a tennis racket.

• Keep sessions short to begin with and don't expect too much too soon. It can take a while for a dog to understand what you want him to do.

• Look for signs that your dog is tired—such as him panting or lying down a lot. He may also just lose interest. Quit while you are ahead and stop the game.

• Not all dogs are keen to fetch. Some much prefer to run away with the toy! If your dog isn't keen, choose a different physical game for him to play (see Chapter 3).

Leave it

Dogs are curious. They sniff and eat pretty much anything—rummaging in a trash can (rubbish bin) is often a favorite activity. They pick up and chew things that don't belong to them, which usually gets them into lots of trouble. Teach your dog to "Leave it" and you'll keep him healthy, safe, and top of the class for good behavior!

The best way to teach a dog to leave something he really wants is to offer him a greater reward. For this training technique you'll need the best and tastiest treats you can find! Leave It requires lots of practice and should be taught in stages —first hold the treat in your hand, then move on to placing it on the floor but covering it with your hand, then, finally, leave it so that your dog can see it.

1 Place something you know your dog likes, such as a dog biscuit, in your hand. Close your hand and allow your dog to try to get to the biscuit. Say Leave it. When he stops trying to get the biscuit and looks at you, praise him, and give him a higher-value treat, such as a piece of chicken or sausage.

2 Once you've practiced step 1 several times, place the biscuit on the floor, and cover it with your hand. Say "Leave it."

Let your dog sniff your hand and try to get to the biscuit. Once he has given up trying to get to the biscuit, praise him, and give him a higher-value treat.

Tips

• Don't be too hard on your dog. He may fail at this many times before he succeeds. The temptation to steal the biscuit may be too much for him!

• Once you and your dog have got this perfect using a biscuit, make the bait more real—for example, empty food packaging that you know he'd love to sniff, lick, and chew.

• Remember to take high-value treats on your walks if you want to practice Leave It when you're out and about.

When you've practiced steps 2 and 3 several times, place the biscuit on the floor so that your dog can see it. Place your hand a few inches above it. Say "Leave it." If your dog leaves it, give him the tastier, higher-value treat.

Drop it

Dogs, especially puppies, will pick up anything that is lying around the house. Items such as your socks, teddy, or favorite magazine will be gone in an instant with a mischievous mutt in the house! Unless you're quick, your precious possessions are likely to be chewed to pieces.

When your dog steals your things, you may be tempted to shout at him and chase him around the house. But if you do this, he'll think it's a game and run away all the more! This is where Drop it becomes very useful. If all goes well with your training, one simple instruction and your item should be returned, undamaged. That's the plan, anyway.

1 Start your Drop It training by using a long sausage dog-type toy or a rope. Allow your dog to pick it up in his mouth and hold the other end yourself.

2 Show your dog that you have a tasty treat on offer. Say "Drop it" and, when he lets go of the toy, give him the treat as a reward.

3 Once you've practiced this with a long toy a few times, use a smaller toy, such as a ball. This time don't hold it yourself. Simply make a fist of your hand, with the treat inside. Hold it below your dog's mouth. Say "Drop it." When the toy drops to the floor, give him the treat.

• Practice Drop It when you're playing Fetch (see pages 60—61).

• Use Drop It when you don't want your dog to take something outside. If he wants to go out, tell him to drop the toy before you open the door. Wanting to go out should be enough to make him drop the item.

SAFETY FIRST

• Never grab a toy from your dog's mouth. This will make him hold onto it even harder. Once he trusts you, he will drop items willingly.
• Always get adult help if you want your dog to drop food. He may become possessive and vicious over something he really wants to eat.
• If your dog begins to growl or stare when you are teaching him Drop It, step away from him. If he has something very valuable to you or dangerous to him, ask an adult to help to get the item from him.

Walking to heel

Will you take your dog for a walk or will he take you?! Many people are pulled along by a dog who hasn't learnt to walk to heel. This technique of walking your dog on a loose leash at your side will make your outings together all the more enjoyable.

1 Put your dog on his leash. Hold the leash in your left hand and a treat in your right hand. Show your dog the treat and let him follow it with his nose until you have him positioned on your right-hand side. Give him the treat.

SAFETY FIRST

• If your dog is medium sized or big and is likely to pull you over, an adult will have to do most of the Walking to Heel training at first.

2 Show your dog another treat and take a step forward. Say "Heel" and, if he stays by your side, reward him with the treat.

3 Next, take two or three steps forward, say "Heel" and give him the treat. Continue with this, taking more steps each time. Tap your right leg as a signal that you want your dog to stay at your side.

4 Make sure the leash is loose at all times. If your dog pulls on the leash, simply stop and tempt him back to the start position.

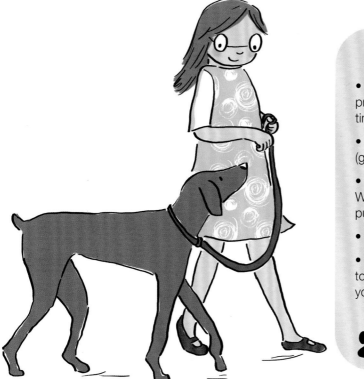

Tips

• Be patient: Walking to Heel training can be a long process, with you having to stop and start several times on a walk.

• Do your first training sessions at home or in the yard (garden) where there are few distractions for your dog.

• Make sure your dog is well exercised before a Walking to Heel training session. He's less likely to pull on the leash if he is tired.

• Praise him as he walks alongside you.

• Most dogs love to sniff and, of course, go to the toilet when they are out. Bear this in mind when you're walking your dog and allow him to do both.

In your bed

Your dog will be your close companion. He will enjoy following you around and sitting with you, but sometimes you will want time out from him. Teaching your dog to go to his own safe place—his bed—is a useful training technique.

It helps if you have already taught your dog to Sit, Lie Down, and Wait (see pages 50—51, 52—53, and 54—55) before you teach In Your Bed.

1 Ask your dog to "Sit" and "Wait" a few feet away from his bed. Kneel down by the bed, show your dog a treat, and then place that treat on his bed.

2 Point to the bed and say "In your bed." Your dog should walk to the bed. Let him eat the treat.

3 When he looks to you for more, tell him to "Lie down," then give him another treat.

4 Spend time stroking him and making him comfortable before you walk away. If he follows you, repeat steps 1—3 again.

Did you know?

You may notice that your dog goes round and round in circles before he lies in his bed, or that he ruffles up a neatly laid-out blanket before lying on it. This behavior is instinctive. It's what your dog would have done if he lived in the wild and had to make his own nest. One theory is that circling would flatten down the surface, such as long grass, and scare away or squash any insects lurking there. Another is that by making a visible nest a wild dog was being territorial and warning off other animals that might be looking for a bed for the night!

 Tips

• Make your dog's bed as comfortable as possible. A puppy, especially, might be more likely to stay in his bed if he has something with your scent on, so give him an item of your clothing to lie on.

• Train your dog to go to his bed when there is nothing that will distract him. Then practice it in different, busier circumstances, such as when guests arrive.

• To begin with, place the bed near to where you are going to be playing, eating, or working on your computer, for example, so that your dog can still see you.

• If you want him to stay on the bed for some time, give him a chew or a hollow toy filled with treats (see page 82).

• Once you've finished your task, go over to him, and give him plenty of praise for staying on his bed.

No jumping

Jumping up to say hello might be cute with a puppy, but when your dog grows up it can be uncomfortable or even dangerous and so is one of the worst habits a dog can learn. If your dog already has this habit, it isn't too late to undo it. Just follow the steps below. Your aim is to keep your dog's four paws firmly on the floor.

Did you know?

Your dog jumps up because he wants to greet you by sniffing your face! This is the technique he uses when he meets other dogs.

1 Teach your dog that there is no reward for jumping up. Simply turn away from him and fold your arms. Don't give him affection or attention as this will encourage the behavior.

2 Once he has four feet on the floor, crouch down, and reward him with a treat and attention. If he tries to jump up in this position, repeat step 1.

SAFETY FIRST

• Bear in mind that a dog that jumps up might really worry friends, especially those who are younger and smaller than yourself, or those who are afraid of dogs.

3 He will eventually learn that you will come down to his level and that he doesn't need to come up to yours. Using the Sit and Wait commands (see pages 50—51 and 54—55) can help, especially if you can't get down to greet your dog immediately.

Tips

• Don't shout at your dog to "Get down" as by doing this you are giving him attention. Although it's difficult, you have to try to ignore him completely.

• Everyone in your house should use this technique. If your dog is allowed to greet some people by jumping up but not others, he will get mixed messages.

• Ask guests to ignore your dog when he jumps up.

• Until your dog has learned not to jump up, don't allow him to go to the door to greet guests. Put him in another room and introduce him to guests when things are quieter and more controlled. It may help to put him on a leash.

Ouch! How to handle play-biting

It is normal for puppies to play-bite. It's how they behave with other puppies when they are play-fighting. However, having your puppy's sharp teeth sink into your hand won't be much fun for you. Even if you don't mind a bit of play-biting, don't allow it. If you let your pup do this once, he will think he can do it all the time.

Try all of the techniques below to stop this bad habit when your puppy is very young. It will take some time for him to learn, but stick with it.

1 Instead of allowing your puppy to play with your hands, use a toy. Hold it and wave it around, encouraging your pup to bite, grab, and wrestle with it.

2 Squeal when you get nipped. This is how another puppy would respond and it will stop your puppy in his tracks.

3 If your puppy tries to play-bite your hand, keep it still and limp instead of moving it around or jerking it away. A still, limp hand won't be of much interest to your playful pup.

4 Encourage licking instead of biting. When your dog licks your hand instead of biting it, give him a treat and praise.

• There is a big difference between a puppy's play-biting and biting and aggression in older dogs. Always get help from an adult if an older dog is being aggressive. Don't attempt to tackle it yourself.

• Never respond to play-biting by hitting your dog. This may make him become aggressive.

• Growling is a warning sign from a dog that he wants to be left alone. Always step away from a dog that is growling.

• Never attempt to do anything to stop dogs that are being aggressive toward each other.

Tips

• Don't point and wave your hands around in front of your puppy. He will think you are playing a game and attempt to bite your hands.

• Don't allow your friends or family members to encourage play-biting. This will give your puppy mixed messages.

• Find opportunities for him to play with other puppies and older, friendly dogs, if possible. This is the best way for your puppy to learn the dos and don'ts of playing.

• Accept that he will chew and ruin soft toys so don't let him get hold of your own favorite ones!

Your sociable dog

Dogs are pack animals so they are naturally sociable and unlikely to enjoy being alone, but your dog may still need your help to become comfortable and well-behaved around dogs and people. A dog that is socialized is less likely to develop problems with his behavior.

SAFETY FIRST

• Always make sure an adult is there when you first begin socializing your dog with your friends and with other dogs.

Meeting your friends

Start by inviting one or two friends over (a larger group of children might be scary for your dog). Walk your dog to the door to greet them, and keep him on a leash if you think he might jump up. Keep some treats by the door and encourage your friends to give a treat to your dog, once he has his four paws firmly on the floor (see pages 72—73) or is sitting. If your dog is nervous, make sure your friends don't overcrowd him. Ideally, go into an open space like a yard (garden) or park and play a fun game, such as Fetch (see pages 60—61).

Arrange to meet your friends when you are out walking. Again, give them treats to give to your dog if he greets them in a friendly way.

Meeting other dogs

Dogs are naturally protective of their own territory, which for your dog will be your house and yard (garden). For this reason, it is best for your dog to socialize with another dog away from your house in a place such as at the park. Allow the dogs to greet each other in a natural way by sniffing each other's faces and bottoms. Begin by keeping both dogs on the leash and walking alongside one another before letting them off the leash to run and play.

Once your dog gets to know another dog, you could arrange a doggy play date at home. Exercise the dogs well first outside the home and then bring them home together, allowing your dog to enter first. It is important that the second dog is clear about whose territory he is entering. Make sure you don't attempt this play date at feeding time, and remove your dog's food bowl from the floor.

Did you know?

Dogs greet each other by sniffing each other's bottoms because the glands in that part of the body give off a strong smell and lots of information. By having a good sniff, your inquisitive mutt can learn the sex of the dog, what he's been eating, and even whether he's likely to be a friendly playmate!

Starting young

• If you have a puppy, give him plenty of opportunities to meet other dogs. Take him to puppy training classes or hang out with friends who have a puppy or an older, friendly dog.

• Get your puppy used to attention by inviting friends over or taking him to places where there are lots of people. Most people—your friends especially—will want to hold and cuddle your puppy but, ideally, they should wait for him to come to them so that it is his choice to have a cuddle.

• Keep meetings short and look out for the body language signs (see page 22) that your puppy may be finding it too much or is tired of being fussed. If your puppy seems nervous of people, give them treats to give to him. He will soon learn to understand that being with humans is a positive and rewarding experience.

• Walk your puppy in different situations and places where he might encounter people with objects such as bikes, strollers (pushchairs), and wheelchairs. These may seem big and threatening to your tiny pup, but the earlier and more often he comes across them, the better. They will become a normal and accepted part of his world.

chapter 3

Fun
and
games

Home-made dog toys

Walk into any pet store and you'll see a big choice of dog toys to buy. Many are over-priced and won't last long, especially if you have a chomping puppy in the house. Why not save your money and make some toys from items around the home?

Sock ball

Socks and balls are often in the top five of a dog's favorite toys, so this is the perfect plaything! Hunt around the house for some odd socks—most families have some—and longer ones are best. Push a tennis ball into the toe of the sock and tie a knot to hold it in place. Swing it around in front of your dog. She'll love the challenge of trying to get a hold of it.

Find the treat

You can buy special toys designed to keep your dog busy. You fill them with treats and your dog has to try to get to the treat. Hours of fun! You can make one yourself using a plastic container, such as a small, empty, plastic juice or water bottle. Use a pair of scissors with pointy ends to make a small hole in the side of the bottle. Now snip around it to make a hole just big enough for a treat to drop through (don't make it too big—the treats should come out gradually). Now open the bottle, put a handful of treats inside, and close it again. As your dog rolls it around, the treats should come out, but be careful. If she starts eating the container itself, you will have to take it from her because the sharp plastic will hurt her mouth.

For a quicker game, put some treats into a cereal box and tape it up. It won't take most dogs long to chew through the box to get to the treats. Expect to have to do some clearing up!

If you have a spare tennis ball, ask an adult to help you make a small hole in one and put treats inside. Your dog will roll the ball around to make the treats fall out.

Tug toy

Get a piece of strong fabric, such as denim or fleece, and a tennis ball. Simply cut three long strips of the fabric, tie them together at the top, and then braid (plait) them. Tie a knot at the bottom. Make quite a big hole in each side of the tennis ball. (You may have to ask an adult with a craft knife to help you do this as tennis balls are quite tough.) Feed the braid through and knot the other end. You can also use a piece of strong rope, instead of making a braid.

Teddy friend

If you have teddy bears or other soft toys you no longer want, give them to your dog. To make them safe, first cut off any small parts such as plastic eyes or ribbons that your dog could choke on or swallow. Watch your dog play with the toy. If she rips it apart, take it away from her because the stuffing can be dangerous.

! SAFETY FIRST

• Always supervise your dog when she is first playing with a new toy to check it is not going to harm her.

Where's the toy?

This game involves hiding your dog's favorite toy and asking her to find it. It's like Fetch (see pages 60–61) but a little more challenging and exciting! Where's the Toy? is a great indoor activity if bad weather stops you going outside.

1 The first step is to make sure your dog loves the toy you are going to hide. Play with it with her beforehand to get her interested and to ensure it has your scent and her own.

2 Start by finding a simple hiding place, such as under the coffee table. Leave a bit of the toy showing.

3 Ask your dog to "Find it." She may need help from you to begin with. If she does, guide her to the toy and point to it, but still praise her when she picks it up. Reward her with a treat.

Tips

• If toys don't interest your dog very much, hide treats instead. Smelly treats such as cooked meat will be most effective, but don't forget to pick them up if your pooch doesn't find them!

• Gradually increase the length of time you leave your dog to look for the toy or treat before helping her. Hunting it down is part of the fun and she'll enjoy the reward of finding it.

• If the weather is good, play Where's the Toy? in the yard (garden). You could hide it behind a bush or in the garage, but make sure she doesn't start digging up your flowers to look for it!

4 Now hide the toy somewhere less visible, such as under a bed. Again say "Find it" and help her hunt it down, if necessary. Praise her and give her a treat when she finds it.

Hide and seek

Turn this into a game of Hide and Seek by hiding yourself with a toy. Get your dog to sit or lie down and Wait (see pages 54—55). Hide behind a door or under a bed with the toy, then shout "Find me!" Your dog will love the reward of finding you and a toy. You can gradually make the challenge harder by hiding in a different room.

Tug-of-war

This is a game that two dogs like to play together. They each have one end of the tug toy in their mouth and pull and pull until one lets go. The rules are slightly different when you play against your dog because you should always win (it's important that your dog sees you as pack leader). It will be just as much fun for your dog, though!

1 Choose a strong tug toy, such as a rope toy, that is long enough to leave a clear gap between your hand and your dog's mouth. Hold one end of the toy in front of your dog and instruct her to "Grab it." She should take hold of the other end of the toy.

SAFETY FIRST

• Your dog may make growling sounds as she pulls, but these should only be playful. If you notice any signs of aggression (see page 22) when you play tug, stop immediately and allow your dog to keep hold of the toy. Don't attempt the game again.
• It's important that your dog understands Drop It (see page 64) before you begin this game as she has to let go when you tell her to.
• Your dog should grab the middle or her own end of the toy and not near to where you're holding the toy.
• Only play this with a specific tug toy, not with very small or soft toys. Never play tug with items of clothing.

2

Let the fun begin. Pull the toy and move it side to side and up and down for around 10—30 seconds.

3

Your dog is unlikely to let go unless you teach her. When you want the game to end, say "Drop it." You may need to show her a treat to tempt her to let go. Eventually, she will learn to drop the toy on the command of "Drop it" only. If your dog pulls the toy out of your hand, instruct her to drop it before you try to take hold of it again. Take a rest before you begin round two!

Obstacle course

Give your dog a physical and mental challenge with this home-made doggy obstacle course. Use as big a space you can find, preferably a yard (garden). Try all the challenges yourself, too. It's fun and a great way to keep fit!

Teach your dog these skills one by one, but work up to getting her to run round the whole obstacle course without stopping.

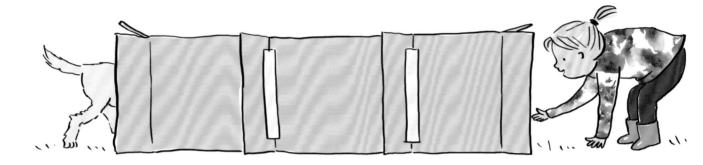

1 **Through the tunnel**
Find three or four large cardboard boxes, all the same size. Open both ends and then tape them together to make a tunnel. Crawl through yourself and encourage your dog to follow you. Once your dog understands what you want her to do, stand at one end and encourage her to run through to the other side. Give her a treat when she reaches you.

! SAFETY FIRST

• Whenever you're playing physical games with your dog, it's important that you both drink plenty of water to avoid dehydration.

Hoops of fun

For this game you'll need a large hula hoop and a friend to help. Your friend should hold the hoop so that it is touching the ground while you walk your dog through it on her leash. When she steps over it, give her a treat. Next, ask your friend to hold the hoop slightly off the ground and encourage your dog to step over it. Once she understands what you want her to do, let her off the leash. Using the treat, encourage her to step or jump over the hoop. Give her lots of praise and the treat when she succeeds. Some dogs really enjoy this game and get very good at it so, with them, you can hold the hoop higher and higher each time.

3 Zig-zag

Place five or six cones on the floor, spaced a few feet apart. If you don't have cones you could use upside-down buckets, flower pots, or even rolled-up clothing. Zig-zag around the cones, encouraging your dog to follow you. Reward her with a treat when she does it. Once you've succeeded in getting her to follow you a few times, set her the challenge of zig-zagging alone. You'll need to run alongside her to encourage her. Give her a treat when she reaches the end. Once your dog is skilled in this, encourage her to dribble a ball around the posts and do the same yourself to improve your soccer skills.

Tips

• Add to the fun and competitive spirit by inviting a friend over with his or her dog. Which dog will win?

• If your dog seems to be naturally good at navigating the course, consider signing her up for agility classes in your neighborhood.

Doggy soccer

Most dogs love to play ball so you shouldn't have difficulty encouraging yours to play soccer. Don't expect her to follow too many rules, though. The emphasis should be on fun!

1 Set up some goals with cones, if you have them, or use items of clothing. Start by encouraging your dog to run between the two goalposts.

2 Then introduce the soccer ball and encourage your dog to chase it, push it along the ground with her nose, and pat it with her feet.

3 If she's learned Leave it (see pages 63—63), use this command when you want to have a turn with the ball.

4 Boost goal scoring by standing behind the goal and encouraging your dog to push or dribble the ball through. Give her a treat and praise when the ball rolls through the goalposts.

Tips

• Don't play Doggy Soccer with your favorite ball because your dog's rough play might burst it.

• If you have a friend with a dog, invite them over for a game!

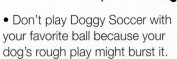

Other sporting challenges

• Your dog can join in your basketball training by standing beneath the hoop to catch or chase the ball.

• If you're playing tennis or baseball, involve your dog by having her fetch the ball for you.

Hidden treasures

Many dogs love to dig but get in trouble for wrecking the lawn and flower beds. If you have a doggy digger, make her a sandbox of hidden treasures to enjoy.

1 For this you will need a children's ready-made sandbox—you may have one you no longer use or perhaps you have some neighbors whose children have grown out of theirs. Place it in the area you want your dog to play in and fill it with sand. It needs to be about 6 in. (15 cm) deep. Sandboxes with lids are best because they can be closed in bad weather and when you don't want your dog to dig.

2 Take your dog's favorite toys and some tennis balls and bury them in the sand. Leave one or two toys unburied on the top to get her started!

3 Encourage her to dig in the sand to find the toys and balls. Praise and reward her with a treat when she finds one.

Tips

• If you don't have sand for your sandbox, use soil or soil and sand, instead.

• Your dog may bark at the box to "tell you" to get the toys for her. Encourage her to hunt them down herself in exchange for treats.

Did you know?

Your dog might be digging because she's hot. Many canines find comfort in the coolness of the dirt (soil) beneath the surface.

Tidy-up time

When playtime is over with your furry friend, there's always tidying up to do. Why not get your dog's help with this by teaching her to put her toys in a container? To be a successful helper, your dog will need to have learnt Fetch (see pages 60–61) and Drop it (see pages 64–65).

1 Throw a toy for your dog to Fetch. While she is running for the toy, place the container by your feet.

2 When your dog returns with the toy, hold your hand over the container and ask her to "Drop." When she releases the toy into your hand, give her a treat and praise.

3 Once she is successfully doing step 2 (this might take several sessions), move to the next stage. This time, drop the treat in the box, instead of giving it to her. She will drop the toy in the container to retrieve the treat.

4 Eventually, she will place the toys in the box without looking for the treat.

 Tip

• Stick with teaching your dog to tidy as it is a hard skill for her to learn. To begin with, she may take more toys out of the box than she puts in.

chapter 4

Clever dog

Teach your dog to wave

Most people find it cute when a dog acts like a human. The Wave trick is guaranteed to impress your friends and make them say "Aaah." Your dog doesn't actually know he's waving—he's just waiting for a treat, but you can keep that part a secret! Make sure your dog will Sit (see pages 50–51) and Wait (see pages 54–55) before you try to teach him to wave.

 Be patient

When you start to teach the tricks in this chapter, always remember that, although the instructions sound simple, you will need to be very patient with your dog and keep practicing every day in short sessions. Don't expect too much too soon or be disappointed with your dog when he doesn't find it easy to learn a new trick. Before you start on tricks, make sure that you have done all the basic training (Chapter 2) and then concentrate on getting him really good at one trick at a time.

1 Hold a treat tightly in your hand and let your dog sniff it. He has to really want the treat for this trick to work.

2 Ask your dog to "Sit." Then sit on the floor opposite him. Place your hand on the floor. Allow him to paw at your hand to try to get to the treat. When he does this, give him the treat.

3 Place another treat in your hand. This time, crouch in front of your dog and move your hand slightly off the floor. When your dog paws your hand, release the treat.

4 Take another treat and this time stand so that your dog has to reach slightly higher to paw it. Give him the treat.

Tips

• Remember that teaching Wave, as with all the tricks in this chapter, should be fun, so keep sessions short.

• Your dog may not always be in the mood to entertain your friends so never force him to wave or do any other tricks.

5 Finally, stand and keep your hand out of your dog's reach so that he paws the air and "waves."

6 Once he has mastered this trick, start to say the word "Wave" when you want him to paw the air. Eventually, he will wave at the sight of your closed fist and the voice command.

Playing dead

Test your dog's acting skills with this fun trick. The aim is to get him to fall from standing to a lifeless lying position with the command "Bang" and a fake "gun"—your hand! This clever prank takes a lot of practice but will really impress your audience if you can pull it off.

1 Tell your dog to "Lie down" (see pages 52—53).

2 Take a treat and hold it in front of your dog's nose. Move it slowly toward your dog's shoulder so that he follows it with his nose and gradually rolls on to his side.

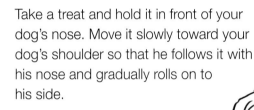

3 Once he's lying on his side, move the treat back to his head and then toward the ground. The aim is to make sure his head is flat on the ground. Once it is, give him the treat.

4 Now stand up and say "Bang," using your hand as a pretend gun. Your dog will probably lift his head up, but only give the treat once his head is resting on the floor.

 Tip

• Practice, practice, practice but only for short sessions. Your dog will eventually learn that he only gets a treat once he's lying on his side with his head resting on the floor— "playing dead."

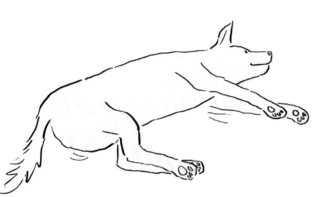

5 When your dog has the hang of this trick, he should fall to the floor from a standing position when you give the hand signal and the command "Bang."

! SAFETY FIRST

• Never push your dog to the ground or place pressure on his head or neck to keep his head flat on the floor.

Roll over

Do you want to show off your doggy's gymnastic skills? Teach him how to roll over with one simple command from you. Make sure you have lots of treats to hand. You'll need to give your dog a tasty reward at each stage of the roll so that he follows your hand with his nose.

1 Begin by asking your dog to "Lie down." Give him a treat.

2 Hold a treat in front of his nose and then move it back toward his shoulder so that he follows its trail and rolls on to his side. Give him the treat.

3 Now move a treat down from his head toward his tail. He will stretch to reach it. Give him the treat.

4 With your dog still lying on his side, move another treat down his body toward his tail, but this time move it over his body so that he has to twist to reach it. The idea is to get him to turn onto his back. Give him the treat.

5 Use another treat to tempt him on to his other side.

6 Once he's learnt to follow the treat, say "Roll over" as you move the treat over his body and he rolls on to his back. Eventually he'll learn that the command "Roll over" means that he has to turn right over onto his front to get the treat.

Tip

• Some dogs don't like lying on their backs, so if your dog seems reluctant, try a different trick or game instead. Don't physically try to roll your dog over.

Did you know?

If your dog rolls onto his back and rubs his shoulders on the ground, it's a sign that he's happy and contented.

High-five

It's cool to have a dog that can "high-five." Once you've trained your dog in this technique, he will be able to greet all your friends in this way. That's pretty impressive!

SAFETY FIRST

• Don't grab hold of your dog's paw or pull his leg during this exercise.

1 Command your dog to "Sit" (see pages 50—51). Sit opposite him on the floor. Hold a treat in your hand and let him paw your hand to get it. Give him the treat.

2 Do the same as step 1 but, this time, hold out your other hand, palm upward, so that he makes contact with that when he tries to paw for the treat. As soon as he taps your empty hand, give him the treat.

Tips

• Move from a sitting to a standing position, so that your dog learns to high-five you in a way that looks more casual than if you are sitting on the floor opposite him.

• If you want to really impress your friends, try the "high-ten." After the first high-five, swap the treat to your other hand and your dog should high-five both hands before he gets the treat.

3 Repeat step 2, but hold your empty hand higher this time.

4 Once your dog is tapping your empty hand each time, move the position of your hand so that your palm is facing toward him. When his paw makes contact with your palm, that's a high-five! Reward him right away.

5 Once your dog has learnt this trick, introduce the command "High-five" when you hold your hand up.

Fetch the leash

As well as being a great companion and entertainer, your dog can be helpful, too. Teaching him to fetch his leash before you go out for a walk will keep him busy while you get ready. This time the reward is very simple—a walk with you! What better feeling is there than being able to get your dog to do as you want?

1 Begin by treating your dog's leash as a toy, something he wants to get hold of. Gently tease him with it and he'll try to grab it. Be careful not to swing it around because, if it harms him in any way, it may become something that frightens him.

2 Once you have your dog's interest in the leash, skim it along the floor and ask him to "Fetch" (see pages 60—61).

Tips

• If your dog is having difficulty holding the leash, tie it in a knot so that it's half the length.

• Make sure his leash is placed somewhere he can get it safely. Drape it over something, rather than placing it on a hook.

• Hang the leash so that the heavy metal clip is close to the floor otherwise when he pulls at the leash it might hit him on his nose!

3 Encourage him to hold it in the middle to make it easier to carry.

4 When your dog returns with the leash, tell him to "Drop it" (see pages 64—65) and reward him with a treat.

5 Once he's got the hang of fetching his leash, show him where it's kept. Stand next to where it is and say "Fetch the leash." Encourage him to pull it down and bring it to you. Eventually, you should be able to say "Fetch the leash" from anywhere in the house and won't need to stand next to it.

 ## More fetch games

• Teach him to fetch other items, such as the mail, a magazine, or your slippers. These won't feel like chores to your dog because he will love to help you.

• If your dog has lots of different toys, teach him their names and ask him to fetch each one individually. You'll have to use the names regularly for him to learn them, so do this daily before you start training him.

Speak (and be quiet!)

Why don't you invite your friends over to have a chat with your dog? The trick is to control your dog's barking and get him to "speak" on command. It is, however, important to balance this new skill with training him how to be quiet!

Dogs bark for many different reasons. For this trick, you're focusing on the bark your dog uses to get attention or when he's playful.

1 Get your dog in a playful mood by showing him his favorite toy. If he isn't that interested in toys, use a treat instead.

2 Tease him a little until he really wants the toy. He will bark to tell you to give it to him. Give him the toy as his reward.

3

This time, do the same as step 2 but say "Speak" before he barks for the toy. As soon as he barks, give him the toy and play with him. He will eventually wait until he hears the command "Speak" before he barks.

Now be quiet!

1 Wait until a time when your dog is barking and say "Quiet." It can help to use a hand signal, such as putting your finger to your lips to say "Shhh," or holding your palm in front of his face.

Tip

• Once your dog has learnt to be "Quiet," you can use this command in other more practical situations, rather than just as a way of entertaining your friends! For example, if someone comes to the door, allow your dog to bark a few times (it's natural for him to guard his territory in this way) but then command him to be "Quiet". Give him a treat when he obeys.

2 As soon as he is quiet, give him a treat. Continue to practice this until he links the command "Quiet" with not barking.

Did you know?

Some dogs "talk" in their sleep because, like humans, they dream. Don't wake your dog at this point—he may be having a very nice dream about chasing rabbits or eating a juicy steak!

Take a bow

So your dog now has a collection of training techniques and tricks under his belt. What better way to end his show than by taking a bow? This simple and very cute trick is really just halfway between standing and Down (see pages 52–53).

SAFETY FIRST

• Your dog won't be comfortable in this position for long periods of time, so keep "Take a bow" training sessions short.

1 Make sure your dog is in a standing position and that you have some treats ready.

2 Holding a treat, move your hand from your dog's nose to the ground.

3 As he follows the treat with his nose, he will lower the front half of his body. When his front elbows and chest are touching the ground and his hind legs are still straight, give him a treat. If he goes straight into a down position, repeat from step 1 again.

4 Once he's in position, ask him to "Wait" for a few seconds to take his applause!

5 Once he has learned how to do this properly, introduce the command "Take a bow."

Tip

• Make an extra big fuss of him at the end of his show. He is a star, after all!

Useful organizations

US

American Kennel Club
A registry of purebred dog pedigrees in the United States.
www.akc.org

ASPCA (American Society for the Prevention of Cruelty to Animals)
An animal welfare charity.
www.aspca.org

Association of Pet Dog Trainers (APDT)
A voluntary organization established to improve the welfare of dogs and the competence of dog owners through the promotion of training skills and techniques.
www.apdt.com

IAABC (International Association of Animal Behavior Consultants)
A professional association for the field of animal behavior consulting.
www.iaabc.org

My USA Pet Supplies
Pet products made in the USA.
www.myusapetsupplies.com

NADOI (National Association of Dog Obedience Instructors)
Certifies dog obedience instructors of the highest caliber, and promotes humane, effective training methods and competent instruction.
www.nadoi.org

Pet Smart
Online pet supplies store.
www.petsmart.com

UK

Association of Pet Behaviour Counsellors (APBC)
An organization that represents a network of animal behavior counselors.
www.apbc.org.uk

Association of Pet Dog Trainers (APDT)
A voluntary organization established to improve the welfare of dogs and the competence of dog owners through the promotion of training skills and techniques.
www.apdt.co.uk

Dogs Trust
The largest dog welfare charity in the UK.
www.dogstrust.org.uk

The Kennel Club
An organization dedicated to protecting and promoting the health and welfare of all dogs.
www.thekennelclub.org.uk

PDSA
The UK's leading veterinary charity.
www.pdsa.org.uk

Pets at Home
Pet care advice and supplies.
www.petsathome.com

Puppy School
An established network of puppy training class tutors.
www.puppyschool.co.uk

RSPCA (Royal Society for the Prevention of Cruelty to Animals)
An animal welfare charity.
www.rspca.org.uk

Index

Acknowledgments

I'd like to thank Cindy, Penny, and Anna at Cico Books for the opportunity to write this book. Thanks to Becky Smith for reading and advising on the text, Susan Akass for her thorough checking and advice, Jane Birch for editing, Hannah George for the wonderful illustrations, and Rosamund Saunders for designing. Thanks to Dr. Kate Borer-Weir, BVSc, PhD, DVA, Dipl ECVAA, FHEA, MRCVS for her veterinary expertise.

Thanks to Mum and Dad for making me the happiest 10-year-old in the world when they gave me my first dog Whiskey, and later my beautiful dog Max. Thanks to Adrian for all his support, as always, and for looking after Liam for a week so that I could finish writing this book. Finally, thanks to Zep (below), my adorable cocker spaniel. I couldn't ask for a more wonderful dog.